ELEPHANT

Written by
Jill Bailey

Illustrated by
John Green

GALLERY BOOKS

An Imprint of W. H. Smith Publishers Inc.

112 Madison Avenue
New York City 10016

This series is concerned with the world's endangered animals, the reasons why their numbers are diminishing, and the efforts being made to save them from extinction. The author has described these events through the eyes of fictional characters. Although the situations described are based on fact, the people and the events described are fictitious.

A Templar Book

First trade edition published in the USA in 1991 by GALLERY BOOKS, an imprint of W.H. Smith Publishers Inc., 112 Madison Avenue, New York, New York 10016.

First trade edition published in Canada in 1991 by W.H. Smith Ltd, 113 Merton Street, Toronto, Canada M45 1A8.

Gallery Books are available for bulk purchase for sales promotions and premium use. For details write or telephone the Manager of Special Sales, W.H. Smith Publishers, Inc., 112 Madison Avenue, New York, New York 10016. (212) 532-6600.

Devised and produced by The Templar Company plc, Pippbrook Mill, London Road, Dorking, Surrey RH4 1JE, Great Britain.

Color separations by Positive Colour Ltd, Maldon, Essex, Great Britain. Printed and bound by L.E.G.O., Vicenza, Italy.

ISBN 0-8317-7830-X

CONTENTS

ON THE ELEPHANT TRAIL

The snow-capped peak of Kenya's Mount Kilimanjaro gleamed in the sunshine as **Paul Steiner** and his assistant, Helen, bumped across the national park in his jeep. Paul had been living in the Kenyan bush, studying elephants, for five years. For some time, he had been following one group of elephants in particular, known as B group. He was recording everything they did or ate. There were eight elephants in the group, led by a female, Bertha, who was probably over 50 years old.

It was early afternoon. Group B had spread out over the grassland to feed, wrapping their trunks around tufts of grass and pulling them out of the ground. It was astonishing how fast they fed. They were pulling up the next tuft while still chewing the last mouthful. Even from a distance, Paul and Helen could hear the rasping sound of their teeth. As the elephants moved they talked to each other in low rumbles.

"Elephants can make sounds so low-pitched that we cannot hear them," said Paul. "We know they can talk to each other when they are at least 2$\frac{1}{2}$ miles apart."

It was very hot. The mountains shimmered in the distance. Bertha gave a loud rumble, and flapped her ears noisily. Instantly, the others stopped feeding and began to follow her.

Elephants once roamed Africa by the million. Now, they are in danger of extinction. The bull pictured above lives in a national park in Kenya.

Left: the African elephant is the largest land animal in the world. The average adult bull stands 11 feet and weighs up to 6 tons.

"Where are they going?" asked Helen.

"To the waterhole," replied Paul. "The younger elephants rely on the older ones to show them the way, and to get them out of trouble. If they are disturbed they will stop and fall silent, then move off swiftly without making a sound. They travel about 3 miles an hour."

7

"Elephants live for a very long time," Paul continued. "They see many things during their lives. That is why it is so sad that the poachers always kill the elephants with the largest tusks, that is, the oldest ones. In parts of Africa only teenage elephants are left. They have no one to show them where to find grazing when the rains fail, and where to find the best grass."

Bertha was enormous, almost 10 feet tall. She must have weighed about 3 tons. Her huge tusks were an amazing 5 feet long.

"Those tusks must be heavy," remarked Helen.

"They are," said Paul, "but her skull is very large and supports very powerful muscles. Part of the

Female elephants live in family groups, and follow their leader to find good grazing or water.

skull is filled with large air spaces, so it is not heavy. She also has a very thick neck."

Suddenly, the B group broke into a run, trumpeting and flapping their ears. They were excited because they could see the water. They rushed in, splashing and sucking up water with their trunks and spraying it over themselves. Their gray bodies turned dark brown.

The youngsters were having great fun. They rolled in the water, spraying each other and tumbling around. The older elephants soon calmed down and began to drink. Belinda's tiny calf knelt down in the water and drank, using his mouth instead of his trunk.

A couple of male elephants wandered up and began to drink. One of the adult females, Bella, snorted angrily and pushed her 12-year-old son, Bertie, out of the way. Then she sidled up to the males, as if wanting to get to know them.

"Bertie is growing up," whispered Paul. "Soon he will have to leave the group and go off on his own with the other males. Adult male

Above: with their supple trunks, elephants throw dust over their bodies. This helps to protect their skin against the sun and insects.

Right: elephants need to drink every day. They do not sweat, so they need to wallow in water or mud to keep cool.

elephants live apart from the females for most of the time."

As the sun went down, the elephants left the waterhole. One of the small elephants was in trouble. She couldn't climb up the slippery bank. She slithered back to the feet of a large male elephant. He looked gently down, then placed his trunk under her belly and lifted her on to the bank.

"Elephants will always help an animal in trouble," said Paul. "They have even been known to help old blind buffaloes. I don't know of any other animals that care so much for their fellow creatures."

Once they were safely on the bank, the elephants began to pick up dust with their trunks and spray themselves with it. They turned a bright red-brown color.

"Why do they do that?" asked Helen.

"Washing and dusting helps to keep their skin cool and moist, and the layer of mud keeps them from getting sunburned. When they rub off the mud later, it will get rid of parasites such as ticks and lice."

Paul and Helen decided to stay by the waterhole to watch the other animals that would come to drink later in the evening.

As the grass grew greener with the spring rains, the elephants wandered away from the swampy area on to the grasslands. Paul and Helen followed them. One day they noticed that 16-year-old Betsy, Bertha's youngest daughter, was lagging behind the others.

Betsy was very restless. Every so often she would stop, pace the ground, and trumpet. She was hardly feeding at all. Paul took a closer look with his binoculars.

"Look," he said, "there is a bulge below her tail."

Finally, Betsy lay down, still trumpeting from time to time. Then she began to study the ground, feeling with her trunk. Her baby had been born.

"It's hairy!" exclaimed Helen.

"Baby elephants are pinkish at first," said Paul, "with tufts of red or black hair. Look at its ears, they look almost transparent."

The baby was very unsteady on its feet. It would be a few hours before it could walk. By now the whole group had come back to admire the new addition. They

Left: cow elephants have two breasts between their front legs. These provide milk for the baby until it is nearly four years old. The cow will continue to suckle until well into her next pregnancy.

Below: newborn elephants can walk within a few hours of birth, but they cannot see very well at first. This cow is guarding a sleeping calf.

would wait for Betsy and her baby. Betsy began to feed and seemed to ignore her tiny baby.

"Betsy is very different from Belinda," remarked Paul. "Belinda knew just how to help her baby to its feet and how to guide it to the milk between her front legs. First babies are more likely to die because their mothers don't know how to look after them."

Two months later, Paul and Helen were watching B group feeding among some trees. Betsy's baby had survived and was trying to pluck some grass. He was not yet in complete control of his trunk.

When they are very tiny, calves may even trip over their trunks. Finally, baby Ben managed to pick up some grass, but he seemed to have forgotten why he wanted it, and placed it on his head.

A couple of male elephants arrived. Immediately, Bella stopped feeding and wandered towards them. The males moved among the B group, feeling them with their trunks. When they came to Bella they became excited, and began to chase her. Bella seemed to have decided she wasn't interested after all, and ran away, trumpeting as she went.

Elephants spend three-quarters of their time feeding. A fully-grown elephant will eat about 370 pounds of grass and leaves a day.

"Bella is in heat," explained Paul. "About two years after the birth of a baby, the mother is ready to mate. This condition lasts for only a few days."

"I didn't see any particular signals," said Helen. "How did the males know she was in heat?"

"She is giving off a particular smell that attracts them, and she has a special rumble to tell them she is in heat," said Paul.

"So why isn't she interested?" asked Helen.

"Elephants can be choosy," said Paul. "She wants to get the best father for her next baby."

The mad chase continued, and over the next few days more males appeared. They were attracted by the rumbling sounds Bella was making. Poor Bella scarcely had a chance to feed or rest.

Male elephants often wrestle or fight, but they do not get hurt. They are testing each other to find out who is the stronger.

One afternoon, Group B suddenly stopped feeding and looked up. They raised their trunks high in the air and sniffed. Over the horizon came a huge bull elephant. Group B rumbled in excitement. As the bull approached, he lowered his head and laid his trunk across one of his tusks. This gesture seemed to reassure Group B who became less agitated. Paul and Helen could smell a sharp odor. Liquid was streaming from behind the bull's eyes, and he was dribbling urine.

"That's Samson," said Paul. "He's in musth – the male equivalent of a cow in heat. Only older bulls over about 30 years of age come into musth. Younger bulls may get to mate with the females, but mating is usually most successful if the bull is in musth."

"Why is he crying?" asked Helen.

"Those are not tears," explained Paul. "There are glands between the eye and ear that produce a special liquid when the elephant is excited."

"How did he know that Bella was on heat?" asked Helen.

"She was calling," said Paul. "Her call was too low for us to hear, but he can hear it from a great distance."

The younger males had retreated into the trees. The bull made straight for Bella, who made no effort to run away this time. He began to feel her with his trunk. Bella backed away and rumbled. Then she reached out her trunk toward him. Soon they were rubbing sides and pressing their heads together. Then Bella turned and backed toward Samson. Trumpeting loudly, Samson began to mate with Bella. Afterwards, the rest of Group B came rushing over, making a great noise in their excitement.

Left: touch and smell play an important part in elephant courtship. A female elephant is most likely to become pregnant if she mates with a male over 30 years old.

Above: bull elephants are much larger than cow elephants. They can weigh up to 6 tons. Their legs form straight, pillar-like supports for carrying this enormous load.

Bella and Samson stayed together for almost three days, mating from time to time. The other males had wandered away. Eventually Samson lost interest in her and went away.

"When will the baby be born?" asked Helen.

"Not for nearly two years," said Paul. "Elephant pregnancies last about 22 months."

They were waiting for Group B to wake up from their midday nap. The elephants were standing in the shade of a large acacia tree, their

Above: the Kenyan grasslands have hot, dry weather. The temperature can be as high as 82° F. Here, elephants stand in the shade of an acacia tree.

Right: an elephant's ears can be nearly 7 feet long and 5 feet wide. As the ears are fanned backward and forward, the blood in them cools. This keeps the body cool.

heads lowered, their trunks almost touching the ground, dozing. The youngsters were stretched out on the ground, sound asleep.

"How do you tell which is which?" asked Helen.

"By their ears," replied Paul. "Each elephant has its own special pattern of veins, and most ears get torn or nicked in time. They also have distinctive tusks. Bertha's tusks are by far the largest. Betsy has broken one tusk. Belinda's are quite curved, while Bella's are almost straight."

"Their ears really are huge," remarked Helen.

"They have very good hearing," said Paul, "but they also use their ears for cooling. The blood vessels come very near the surface of the skin. As they flap their ears, their blood loses heat, so cooling down the body. They also use their ears to fan cool air over themselves."

All at once Group B woke up. Their ears pricked and they sniffed the air with their trunks. Bertha trumpeted loudly, and so did Belinda. The youngsters stood up. Then they all galloped madly towards the distant mountains.

"Something has frightened them," said Paul. "I hope it's not poachers."

ELEPHANTS IN DANGER

Moses Munguti turned to his young son, David, and warned him to be very quiet. He was teaching David about life in the bush, and had brought him along to track Group B. Paul Steiner had told him of the elephants' fright the day before, and Moses wanted to look for the cause.

Moses was a ranger with the national park service. In 1979, there had been 1.3 million elephants in

Typical dry acacia savannah, the home of the bush elephant. The winds carry rain to these grasslands only in the spring and summer.

Africa. Just ten years later, there were only about 600,000. Poachers were killing up to 100,000 a year for their ivory tusks. In another ten years the African elephants could be extinct. Moses wanted to make sure that Group B were safe. They were following the elephants' tracks – and their huge droppings.

"I bet you could see these from an airplane," remarked David.

"You can," said Moses. "In fact, we use the droppings to tell us where the elephants are when the bushes are too thick for us to see the animals ourselves."

With its huge ears spread wide, its large feet pounding the ground, and its tusks lowered to attack, an angry elephant looks terrifying.

"Why do they make so much?" asked David.

"The plant food they eat is hard for them to digest," said Moses, "and a lot of what they eat just passes straight through. They have to eat a lot of food to get the nourishment they need."

"Look!" whispered David, pointing. "There are the elephants."

They could just make out Group B in the distance. They were not feeding. As Moses and David crept forward, there was a thundering of feet and Bertha burst through the bushes, trumpeting loudly. Her ears were spread wide.

David and Moses ran back to their jeep. Angry elephants are very dangerous. They can toss a man high in the air or impale him on their tusks. Bertha followed them, but stopped just short of the jeep. After a few angry snorts she turned and ambled away.

"She doesn't usually act like that," said Moses. "She knows me. Something must be wrong." He reached for his binoculars. Group B were clustered around something on the ground. Moses and David drove to a place where they could get a better view.

An orphaned elephant is usually adopted by the rest of the group. Elephants care for each other when they are in trouble, but orphaned babies seldom survive.

It was a dead elephant. Moses could see that it was Bella. Her face was horribly scarred. Most of it had been cut away, together with the tusks. Bella's three-year-old calf was prodding her body with his foot, and trying to suckle. Belinda was trying to move him away with her trunk.

The elephants' distress was easy to see. Liquid streamed down their faces. They paced the ground, unwilling to leave Bella. Eventually they began to kick earth over the body. They kicked up twigs and branches and covered her.

"They're burying the body," said David, amazed.

Poachers kill elephants for their ivory tusks. The tusks are then sold to people who make them into trinkets, jewelery and ornaments.

"Elephants are the only animals who seem to understand death," said Moses. He remembered the times when he was younger, when he, too, had killed elephants for their tusks. He had never stayed around to see the elephants' grief. He had never understood how human their emotions were.

"Come on," he said to David, pretending not to notice the tears trickling down the boy's face. "Let's go home."

Moses and David drove home. "What will happen to Bella's baby?" asked David.

"I'm afraid that it will probably die," said Moses, angrily.

"Won't the others look after it?" asked David.

"One of the other females will care for it, but none of them has enough milk to spare," said Moses. "Both Belinda and Betsy have new babies of their own to feed, and Bella's baby will probably need milk for another year yet."

"But I've seen it eating grass," said David, hopefully.

"Baby elephants need milk as well as grass for three or four years," said Moses, "and there are lions, hyaenas, and other animals waiting to pounce on orphan elephants."

"So the poachers have really killed two elephants," said David.

Park rangers on patrol in Kenya. The rangers often come from local villages. They are provided with uniforms, vehicles, and guns. Protecting elephants is an expensive operation.

"No, three," said Moses. "Bella was pregnant."

"Tosh's father was shot for poaching elephants," said David. Tosh was his best friend.

Moses had been with Tosh's father at the time, but had managed to escape. The Kenyan government had ordered the rangers to shoot poachers on sight because several rangers had been killed in shootouts with poachers. It was thought to be the only penalty likely to stop criminals from killing the elephants.

After his friend's death, Moses had given up poaching. The rangers had not recognized him, and he had been able to get a job as a porter, carrying the luggage of tourists visiting the park. He learned more about the wildlife of the park by listening to the guides, and had come to love the gentle elephants.

Baby elephants need a lot of help. They cannot even control their own trunks for about six months, and will stay with their mothers for up to 12 years.

David was upset about Tosh's father being killed.

"Tosh says it isn't right to take a man's life for killing an elephant. He says men are worth more than elephants. Tosh's mother has to go out to work to feed her family."

"Men like Tosh's father don't really deserve such tough punishments," said Moses. "He only wanted a better life for his family. You must remember, though, that Tosh didn't die, but that baby elephant will. The large ivory gangs, on the other hand, think nothing of killing rangers, or anyone, who gets in the way.

"These large gangs of poachers are the real problem. They come in from Somalia and other countries with their machine guns. They would have killed the whole elephant family, including the babies – every elephant in sight. They are killing nearly 300 elephants a day in Africa. Soon there will be no elephants.

"It's not only the elephants that

Above: these rangers have discovered a deserted poachers' camp. Quite often the poachers bury the tusks and return later.

Left: as the largest elephants are killed, more and more elephants with smaller tusks are needed to produce the same amount of ivory, so the slaughter gets worse.

die. Hundreds of rangers have been killed by poachers. These men also have families."

"What would happen if all the elephants went?" asked David.

"The tourists would not come to our country," said Moses. "Lots of jobs would be lost and the parks would soon become farmland, even though these areas are really too dry. The cattle would multiply and the grass would all be eaten. This place would soon be like a desert.

"Surely it makes more sense to keep the wild places and the wild animals and make a good living from them."

Moses turned the jeep around. "Let's go up to the top of that hill over there," he said. "It is one of my favorite places."

They reached the top of the hill. The national park spread out below them. It was a vast expanse of golden grassland with dark flat-topped acacia trees and gleaming waterholes. Moses pointed to some wide tracks criss-crossing the grassland.

"Those are elephant roads," he said. "They have used the same paths for hundreds of years, even in dense forest. By keeping the paths clear, they open up the bush for lots of other animals to move through. Elephants need a large area of bush to survive. Every few years there is a drought, and they need to travel long distances to

As an elephant family moves from one part of the bush to another, they keep to paths that are hundreds of years old. These paths are also used by other animals.

find food. If they are fenced in, they may starve.

"Look at those waterholes," he continued, and pointed to three waterholes in a dry river bed. "The elephants made those. There was no surface water there, but they dug with their tusks until they reached the water far below, then they trampled the ground to squeeze the water out of the earth.

"Now other animals can share the water, so they can use the surrounding areas of the bush for feeding. Without the elephants, a lot of other wildlife – giraffes, antelopes, zebras, gazelles, warthogs, and all the animals that feed on them, the lions, cheetahs, leopards, hyaenas, and jackals – would also disappear."

Waterholes are essential to animal life in a country where there are long periods of drought. Elephants often make these waterholes. Here, zebras, ostriches, and gemsboks have gathered to drink.

Above: game reserves and national parks attract tourists from all over the world. The money these people bring to the area can benefit a large number of local people. Poaching brings money to only a few.

Right: an elephant's tusks are actually incisor teeth. They continue to grow throughout the animal's life. The molar teeth are gradually worn away. In a lifetime, an elephant will grow six sets of teeth.

The sun was setting. Moses and David watched the animals moving towards the waterholes. There were tall giraffes, zebras, and stately herds of elephants. David pointed at some large birds circling in the crimson sky.

"Look at those big birds over there," he said.

They were vultures. That meant there must be a carcass below. Moses searched with his binoculars. He found the spot – beneath the vultures was a freshly killed elephant.

"We must hurry back to headquarters," he said. "Those poachers mean business."

As they drove along, David asked, "Does ivory make a lot of money?"

"Yes," replied his father. "One big tusk would bring in more than I earn in a year. Of course the elephant is then dead, and no more money will be made from it. A living elephant brings in about $15,000 a year from tourists, while its ivory is worth just a single payment of about $1,800."

"What exactly is ivory?" asked David.

"It's the elephant's front teeth," said Moses. "Tusks are really long teeth. The trunk is the nose and upper lip joined together. It's strange to think that men risk their lives just to get hold of an animal's teeth, isn't it?"

"How do elephants eat, then?" asked David.

"Elephants have other teeth for chewing with. In fact their cheek-teeth are enormous. The sixth and last pair are the biggest: each tooth weighs about 10 pounds. As the teeth wear down, the elephants grow new ones."

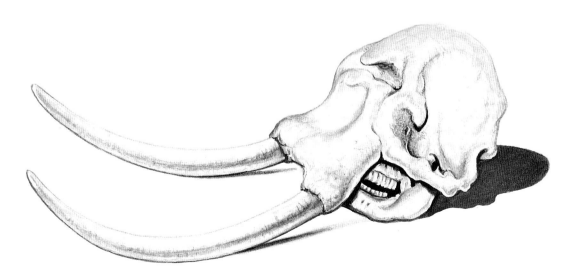

A large group of rangers set out at dawn, planning to ambush the poachers at their hideout. They found the camp not far from the second dead elephant. The poachers were sleeping in the hollowed-out trunk of an old baobab tree.

The rangers, all armed, surrounded the tree very quietly, then called to the poachers to surrender. Two heads appeared, then the men emerged, hands above their heads. Moses sighed with relief. He hated shoot-outs. It reminded him of the death of his friend not so long ago.

Before they had reached headquarters with their prisoners, a radio call had come through. Paul

Steiner had been making an aerial survey of the elephants from his airplane, and had spotted many corpses and groups of fleeing elephants in a far corner of the park. The Somali raiders had struck again.

These gangs were heavily armed and very dangerous. Sometimes the park had to call in the army to help deal with them. If they could find their camp they might even fire a rocket at it rather than approach it and risk the rangers' lives.

Such operations are very expensive and use money the park would rather spend on improving facilities for tourists. Fortunately, many international wildlife organizations send money to help

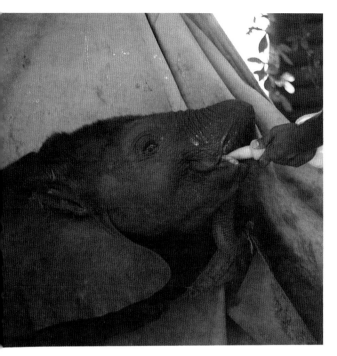

pay for the equipment used by the anti-poaching patrols.

It was going to be a long, hard and dangerous day. The African rangers are brave men – they risk their lives to save the elephants.

Below: the old baobab tree had been hollowed out by elephants, who like to eat its juicy pith. This is where the poachers had been hiding.

Above: orphaned calves sometimes have to be cared for by humans. They do not always take easily to milk which is not elephant's milk.

THE
IVORY WAR

Douglas Holroyd was writing a book on the problem of elephant poaching. He had soon found himself in the middle of a war. He had been threatened, physically attacked, and his camera had been smashed. His work was far more dangerous than he could have imagined. There was so much money in the ivory business that certain people would do anything to avoid being discovered.

The ivory trade only became a serious threat to the elephants in the 1970s. A sudden shortage of oil caused the world economy to collapse, and ivory became more valuable than gold. The price of ivory soared, and poaching began to be organized on a massive scale.

Douglas was now in Dubai, on the coast of the Persian Gulf. To control the trade, most African countries had imposed strict limits on the amount of ivory that could be exported. Dubai had not, so much illegal ivory was smuggled from East Africa to Dubai.

Some businessmen from Hong Kong and Taiwan had set up factories in Dubai, carving illegal ivory. Then they exported it legally to the Far East.

Above: large quantities of illegal ivory are confiscated before they reach the countries where they are carved and sold to dealers.

Left: after dark, dhows *loaded with poached ivory sneak out of East African ports and head for Dubai.*

Douglas and his cameraman friend, Alistair, found one factory in a dirty side street leading off the main market. They crept around to the back of the building, and found the door ajar. Inside there were tusks of all sizes stacked around the walls. Several men sat at long benches working the ivory with electric-powered carving tools. In another corner were crates of ivory. These were ready to be shipped to Hong Kong.

Alistair's camera clicked again and again. As he pointed it at the piles of ivory a shaft of sunlight flashed on its metal case. In a moment, two of the men leapt up and were rushing towards them. As Douglas and Alistair sped down the street, other men appeared from alleyways, carrying heavy sticks. They were almost upon them when

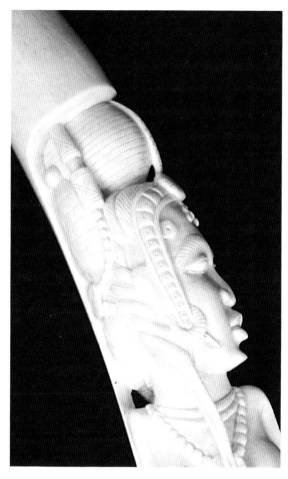

Above: ivory is highly prized for its beauty, its pale shine, its smooth surface, and the ease with which it can be carved into delicate patterns.

Left: Douglas and Alistair fled down the street. There is a lot of money to be made from illegal ivory. The men with the sticks would stop at nothing to protect their interests.

Douglas and Alistair reached their car, leapt in, and roared away.

"Who were they?" gasped Alistair.

"The ivory mafia," said Douglas. "The dealers are in league with the Triads, a kind of Chinese mafia. They have plenty of hitmen to deal with troublemakers like us."

A few days later, the Dubai government announced that it had decided to join the ban on illegal ivory imports.

"What will happen to that factory?" asked Alistair.

"The business will move to another country where the rules are not too strict," said Douglas.

Douglas and Alistair flew on to Zimbabwe to visit some wild game ranches, where local people help to protect wildlife. These ranches have large populations of elephants, antelopes, and other large animals. Hunters pay huge sums of money, up to $30,000, to come and shoot selected animals. Much of this money now goes to the local communities.

The elephants are so numerous that some are shot for their ivory, which is also sold. The meat from elephants and antelopes is sold to local villages. The ranches bring in so much money for local people that there are very few poachers in those parts of Zimbabwe.

Douglas talked to one of the ranch managers.

"You know there is likely to be an international ban on importing ivory goods," he said.

"We are very worried about that," replied the manager. "We would not agree to it. After all, our system of saving the elephants works very well. The elephants we shoot are carefully selected so as not to upset the numbers of males and females. It's not like poaching, where you end up with herds of aimless teenagers. South Africa and Botswana have large herds of elephants on ranches, too."

"It does seem unfair," said

Douglas, "but as long as there is a legal market for ivory, illegal ivory will be passed off as legal ivory. At the moment 80 percent of all legal ivory starts off as poached ivory. So the poaching will continue."

When Douglas got back to his hotel, he found an urgent message. He was to go to Kenya immediately. The President, Daniel arap Moi, was planning to burn 12 tons of confiscated ivory, worth over $2.7 million, to try to persuade other countries to ban the ivory trade.

Tourism was such an important part of Kenya's economy that the President felt that such a sacrifice was worth making.

It was a spectacular bonfire and Alistair managed to get some very dramatic pictures.

"Many people will no longer buy things made of ivory," said Douglas as he and Alistair watched the flames. "Hopefully, one day the market for ivory goods will disappear and the elephants' tusks will be worth nothing."

Left: in July, 1989, President Daniel arap Moi of Kenya burned 12 tons of confiscated ivory as a protest against the ivory trade.

Below: in Zimbabwe, South Africa, and Botswana, elephants are farmed on ranches. This makes money for local people.

39

Douglas then traveled on alone to Hong Kong, to visit one of the oldest and most skilled carvers of ivory. The old man was working on a piece of ivory when Douglas arrived, but there were no piles of tusks to be seen.

"How much ivory do you use?" asked Douglas.

"Only about two tusks a year," said the old man. "The work I do is so fine and takes so long that I have no need of more."

"Many countries are planning to ban the import of ivory objects," said Douglas. "What will happen to your business then?"

"Here in Hong Kong we have nearly 700 tons of ivory stockpiled," replied the old man, "so we shall not run out of supplies. I shall still sell my carvings to the people who live here, but tourists will not be able to take them home. That will hit the manufacturers of mass-produced ivory ornaments.

"The Japanese are the manufacturers' most important customers," he continued. "They use ivory *hankos* – small carved blocks – which they place on an inkpad, then press on to paper to sign their names. This is considered much superior to signing your name with a pen.

"The Japanese also like to wear ivory toggles on their *kimonos*.

Some of these toggles are very finely carved with small figures and traditional designs. Not all these are made in Hong Kong. Many are carved in Japan."

In Hong Kong, Douglas visited one of the oldest and most skilled carvers in the city. His carvings were beautiful, but how could anyone be sure they were made from legal ivory?

Hong Kong has been called "the ivory capital of the world," because so much of the world's ivory finds its way there to be carved or sold.

While Douglas was in Hong Kong, many countries signed an agreement to ban the import and export of ivory and ivory carvings. Even Hong Kong and Japan signed, although Hong Kong later backed out because it wanted to use up its huge stocks of ivory.

Douglas visited a Japanese ivory dealer, Mr Mitsuko, to find out how the ban would affect him.

"Well," said Mr Mitsuko, "of course we shall lose money. We are trying to find other materials that look like ivory and carve well. Some plastics may be suitable, but they do not have the fine grain of ivory. Walrus tusks are better."

Douglas shuddered. So the walruses would now be slaughtered just like the elephants.

"It would be better to change the fashion for ivory *hankos*," he said.

Four months later Douglas, Paul, and Moses were watching the elephants at a waterhole. Douglas asked if the poaching had slowed down since the ivory ban.

"Very much so," said Paul. "We have lost only 18 elephants in the whole of Kenya so far this year. There has been an increase in poaching again since Hong Kong lifted its ban. I guess some illegal ivory is still getting through, but the price of ivory has almost halved."

"It must be tough on Zimbabwe," remarked Douglas. "After all, producing enough elephants to be able to afford to kill some was a good way to save them."

Moses Munguti thought of the day he and his son had found the dead Bella. He remembered how distressed the elephants had been.

"It doesn't seem such a good idea to me," he said.

Elephants are popular with visitors to zoos. Nothing, however, can replace the sight of elephants roaming freely in the grasslands and forests of their natural habitat.

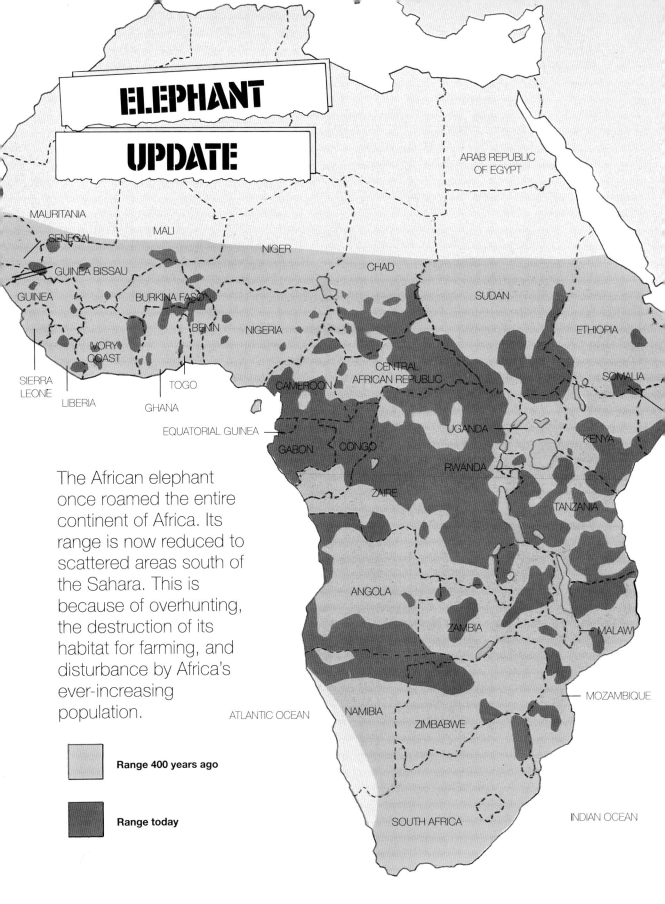

ELEPHANT
UPDATE

ARAB REPUBLIC
OF EGYPT

MAURITANIA

SENEGAL

MALI

NIGER

CHAD

SUDAN

GUINEA BISSAU

GUINEA

BURKINA FASO

BENIN

NIGERIA

ETHIOPIA

IVORY
COAST

SIERRA
LEONE

TOGO

LIBERIA

GHANA

EQUATORIAL GUINEA

CAMEROON

CENTRAL
AFRICAN REPUBLIC

SOMALIA

UGANDA

KENYA

GABON

CONGO

RWANDA

ZAIRE

TANZANIA

The African elephant
once roamed the entire
continent of Africa. Its
range is now reduced to
scattered areas south of
the Sahara. This is
because of overhunting,
the destruction of its
habitat for farming, and
disturbance by Africa's
ever-increasing
population.

ANGOLA

ZAMBIA

MALAWI

MOZAMBIQUE

ATLANTIC OCEAN

NAMIBIA

ZIMBABWE

Range 400 years ago

Range today

SOUTH AFRICA

INDIAN OCEAN

The African elephant

This is the largest species of elephant, standing up to 11 feet tall and weighing up to 6 tons. Its pinkish-gray skin has very little hair. The skin may look a different color after a dusting with sand. It has a low forehead, and its back dips in the middle. The trunk has two lips at the tip. Both male and female African elephants have large tusks.

There are two races or subspecies of African elephant – the forest elephants and the savannah elephants. On the whole, forest elephants are found only in dense forest. They are smaller than their savannah cousins, at most 8 feet tall, and they have smaller ears. Their tusks are straighter and more slender, and point downward. This means that they do not get tangled up in the undergrowth.

AFRICAN ELEPHANT

The Indian or Asian elephant

The Indian or Asian elephant's range, which extends from India to China and the islands of Indonesia, has been reduced to isolated patches of hill country in areas that are difficult to farm. The Indian elephant reaches a height of only 10 feet, and weighs up to $5\frac{1}{2}$ tons. Its skin is similar in color to that of the African elephant, but becomes blotchy pink with age. This species has a very high forehead, and its back is humped. The trunk has a single lip at its tip. Only the males grow large tusks. In females the tusks seldom grow long enough to protrude below the lips.

INDIAN OR ASIAN ELEPHANT

INDEX